Copyright © 2023 by Dian Brand

All rights reserved. No part of this book may be reproduced or transmitted in any form or by any means without permission in writing from the publisher.

www.innovatorspioneers.com

Innovators and Pioneers

Neil Armstrong

Written by Diane Z.
Illustrated by Paulina Zawiska

Neil Alden Armstrong was born in Wapakoneta, Ohio. He grew up in a small town and always had a passion for flying.

He loved building model airplanes and dreaming about flying in the sky.

Neil worked hard to make his dream come true. He learned to fly when he was just 16 years old, receiving his pilot's license even before his driver's license.

After flying fighter jets for the Navy, Neil became an astronaut for NASA. He was determined to be part of an exciting new mission to take people to the moon.

The most important moment in Neil's life came, he was chosen to be the commander of the Apollo 11 mission.

The mission was to land on the Moon, something that had never been done before. Neil, along with his team set out on this amazing journey.

Before going to the Moon, astronauts had to practice "walking on the Moon." Wearing heavy spacesuits, Neil and his team trained in a giant swimming pool and practiced moving around in water.

When Neil and his team flew into space on their way to the Moon. They looked out of the spaceship's window and saw a beautiful blue planet!

The journey to the Moon took several days. Neil and his team ate special space food, and slept in cozy sleeping bags that stuck on walls so they didn't float away.

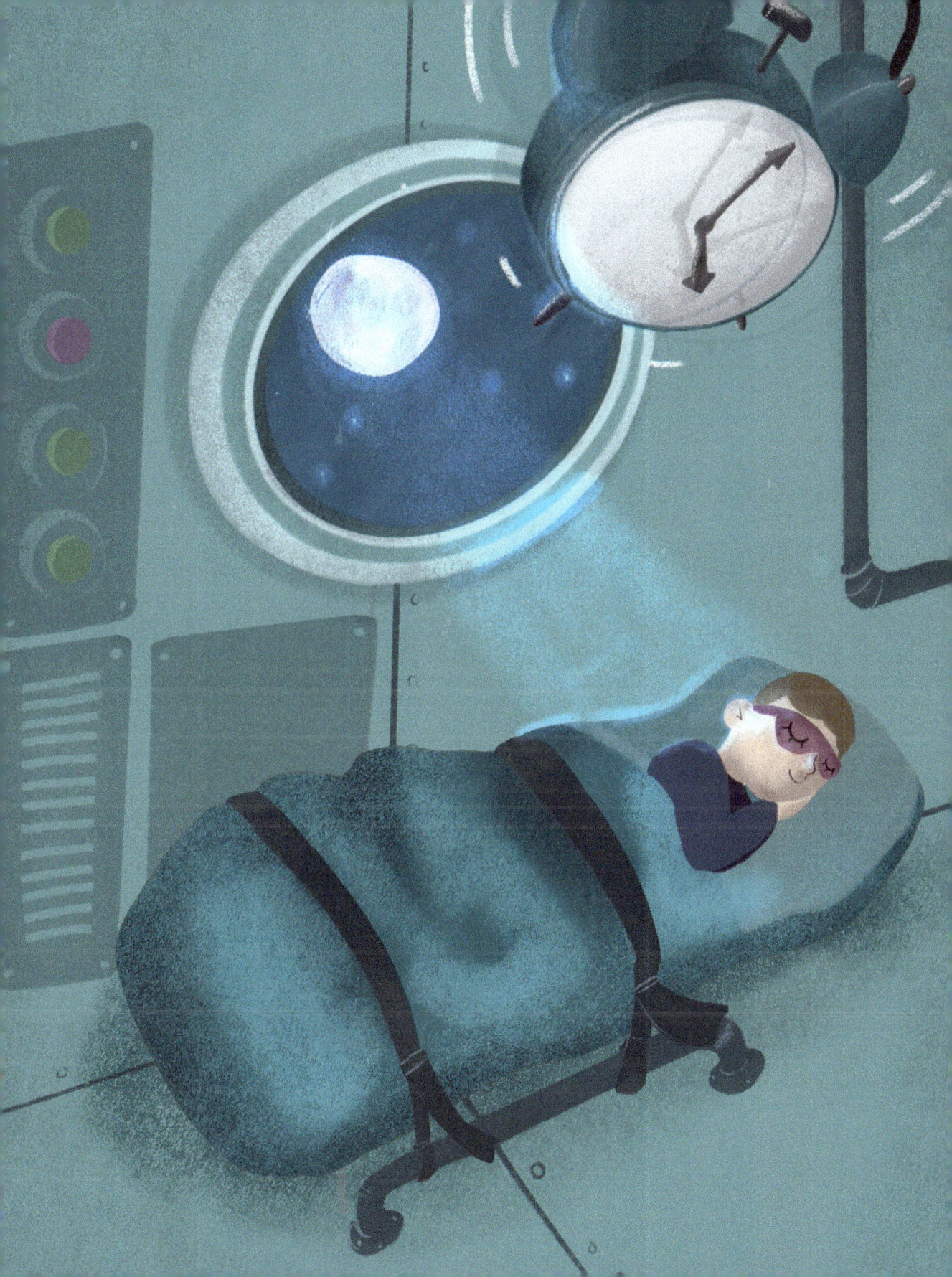

On July 16th, 1989, the Apollo 11 spacecraft arrived at the Moon! Neil and his team got into a smaller spacecraft and descended on the Moon's surface.

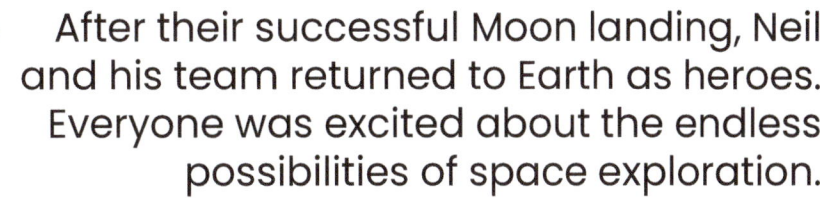

After their successful Moon landing, Neil and his team returned to Earth as heroes. Everyone was excited about the endless possibilities of space exploration.

Cheered as a hero, Neil stayed humble and always attributed the successful Moon mission to the thousands of people who worked at NASA.

MAN ON MOON

Awesome N

After his space adventures, Neil became a professor. He loved sharing his knowledge with young people and inspiring them to reach for the stars.

Neil continued his love for model airplanes. He was a founding member of the Sky Kings and Soaring Eagles model airplane clubs, where he enjoyed socializing with other enthusiasts.

Neil Armstrong will forever be remembered as a hero. He was the first person to walk on the Moon, a pioneer in space exploration, and an inspiration to all who dream of reaching for the stars...

www.ingramcontent.com/pod-product-compliance
Lightning Source LLC
Chambersburg PA
CBHW061403010526
44119CB00010B/246